Published in France under the title *Antranik et la Montagne Sacrée*
© Flammarion 1978
First published in Great Britain 1979
English translation © J.M. Dent & Sons Limited 1979
All rights reserved
Printed in Italy for
J.M. Dent & Sons Limited
Aldine House Albemarle Street London
ISBN 0 460 06877 6

Devis Grebu

ANTRANIK
and the Mystic Mountain

An Armenian Folk Tale

Retold by Nane Carzou
Translated by Gwen Marsh

J.M. Dent & Sons Limited
London   Toronto   Melbourne

In a far away country long, long ago, there was a king named Aldebrank who ruled a tiny Balkan kingdom which is not found in our atlases today. It disappeared from the map many centuries ago. Aldebrank had two brave sons who did all they could to help him rule wisely and well.

One day the King fell very ill. The most learned doctors came to his bedside and examined him with thorough care. One used leeches to bleed him, the second advised baths, while the third made him drink a potion of crushed rhubarb leaves in Tokay wine. As none of these remedies brought relief to the King, an old witch-like woman was sent for who lived in a cave in the Black Mountain.

She came wearing a red shawl wrapped round her head and face so that all that showed was her long nose and her piercing black eyes. Approaching the King she gazed at him for a long time, muttering the strangest sounds: 'Bil-bol-crat-crat, vi-di-ni-boom-boom-boom, ta-ra-ra-ar-cha-da-qua-qua-qua?', then, raising her head, she declared: 'This illness calls for a magic medicine. King, you shall be cured the day you touch a piece of the holy ark in which Noah saved all the animals from the Flood.

The ark came to rest on Mount Ararat.' With these words the old woman vanished as a nightmare does when you awake. The King's sons, Balthegor and Antranik, were bewildered and wondered if they had been dreaming.

'Where,' they asked, 'is this Mount Ararat – if it even exists?'

The King's geographer was consulted but could only bleat: 'Hm . . . er . . . I'll look into the matter . . .' and he disappeared into his study which was cluttered with all sorts of instruments.

Four days later he reappeared before the two Princes looking very wise. 'Ararat rises to a height of almost seventeen thousand feet in a large kingdom called Armenia. To get there one must cross Bielogastan, then the sea, then part of Asia Minor and Anatolia. It will be a long journey.'

Antranik, the younger prince, thought for a moment then spoke as follows: 'Our father is ill and we must cure him. So we must at all costs find the remains of that famous ark. One of us must stay here to help him. You are the elder and therefore the wiser, Balthegor, so you can help him best.'

Balthegor agreed to his young brother's suggestion. 'You are right, you are younger than I am, therefore stronger and quicker. You shall go on the journey while I stay here to be with our father.'

It took three days and three nights for Antranik, with the geographer's help, to work out the details of the route which would bring him to the Mystic Mountain. After saying farewell to his father and promising solemnly to bring back a piece of Noah's Ark, Antranik leapt on his black thoroughbred, Chernego. His squire, Simitrol, rode behind him with all the luggage on a big bay horse.

For five whole days their journey was easy and uneventful. Peasants gave them all they needed in the way of food for themselves and their horses. On the evening of the sixth day they found themselves in a little

6

village on the shore of the Black Sea. They decided to rest there before making inquiries about the crossing. The next day, refreshed and ready, they began asking people where they could find a boat, but nobody knew.

Then an old man with a long grey beard and a turban on his head ventured a suggestion.

'When I was a boy I heard my parents talk of an amazing magician who lived not far from our village and who could grant anything you wished. But it seems he was so hideously ugly that anyone who went to him was frightened out of his wits at the sight of him, so no one ever had a wish granted.'

Antranik threw a purse full of gold to the old man by way of thanks and leapt into the saddle. The faithful Simitrol followed suit and both searched the woods for miles around. But they found nothing. As dusk approached they began to feel discouraged. But all at once the black horse pricked up his ears and, uttering a plaintive whinny, raked the earth nervously with a hoof.

'Stop a moment,' murmured Antranik, 'my horse must have sensed something . . .' Straining their ears they caught the sound of moans broken by gasps and sobs. It was a sound most terrible to hear. Antranik rushed towards the bushes from which these inhuman sounds seemed to be coming. Brave though he was, he stopped short in his tracks at the sight that met his eyes. What looked like an enormous blackish spider was struggling in the threads of a monstrous web. Daring to take a closer look at this monster he saw that in fact it was half human, for its head had a brow, two eyes, a mouth, a nose and two ears like everyone.

'What a hideous creature! One wouldn't have thought such a thing possible!' exclaimed the young man.

Beneath a very narrow brow were two tiny but extraordinarily bright eyes gazing from cavernous hollows. It was as if the creature were looking at you from inside his hideous skull. The nose was very fat, resembling a huge pepper cut in two and curling itself comically round the ears. And what ears! Say rather two trumpets, so long that they touched what might have passed for shoulders on a human being. As for the mouth, the very thought of it made the onlooker sick. It was small with four long stumps of teeth that bit into the thin lips. The body was like a spider at least six feet tall, and this vile spider was writhing in the threads of its web.

Overcoming his fears, Antranik went closer and saw that the threads were really black snakes that were weaving themselves ceaselessly in and out and thus were strangling their prisoner more and more tightly.

At last the Prince cried: 'Who are you and what can I do for you?'

'Have pity and save me from these monsters first: when they are all dead, then I will tell you who I am.'

Night had already wrapped the forest in darkness, but Antranik was not to be put off. He drew his sword and rushed upon the web. The first blow killed twelve black snakes whose severed parts continued to writhe upon the ground. With the second stroke of the sword, eight more reptiles had the life struck out of them. But they seemed to multiply again as quickly. All Antranik could make out was a seething, crawling mass. He called on Simitrol to help him and both fought fiercely for a long time until at last they stopped, exhausted. An unreal light bathed the tree which had held the web – but the web had disappeared. Standing in the beam of this strange light was a man in the prime of life, dressed in plum-coloured velvet with an elegant fan-shaped beard falling down over his chest.

He smiled at them. 'I can never thank you enough. You have saved more than my life. I am the famous magician, Alexiano-Vocheyin. Because I

displeased my supreme master he sent me away in disgrace to live near a poor village, far from my home. I had to accomplish at least one miracle in the next hundred years, otherwise I would be slowly choked by my master's special cobras. I possessed the power to fulfil even the most fantastic of men's desires but the shape and looks my master had given me inspired such fear and loathing that no one could bear to look at me. The peasants ran away and I could never do anything for them. I survived, though my strength was ebbing little by little. Yet I still hoped against all hope. And then you came! You saved me! What can I do for you? Say and it shall be done, for I have not lost my magic power.'

He clapped his hands and a splendid tent of blue brocade rose among the trees. Antranik stepped inside and saw two beds, a table groaning under the weight of delicious dishes of food and, beyond, a manger full of fresh hay and a great trough of pure water for the horses.

Marvelling, he cried, 'What wonderful luck! You are the very man to help me.' He told him his story and ended by saying, 'So what I need, you see, is a good ship in which to cross the Black Sea.'

'Nothing simpler, my friend. I am the man to help you. For the present, eat and sleep. Tomorrow you shall have all you desire.'

The two companions busied themselves first with their horses, then, when they too in their turn had eaten well, they went to bed and slept soundly.

The next day they awoke feeling cheerful and refreshed. The forest had disappeared and in its place was a shore where the blue waves lapped. They were alone, the horses were no longer there, but a beautiful ship, well-built and brightly painted, rode at anchor, rocking to the rhythm of the waves. Close by stood Alexiano-Vocheyin smiling.

'Have no fear. I will take your horses across. When you reach the other shore they will be waiting for you, ready to share your adventures. You will be in a country conquered by barbarians who squeeze the cruellest taxes out of the people. Their descendants will overrun Constantinople in the fifteenth century and will earn the hatred of future generations by their cruelty. Beware, never provoke them. In case you should fall into their hands, I am going to give you an Armenian mushroom; it is no ordinary mushroom for it will make you invincible. The natives of my country — far-off Cappadocia from which my master banished me — put this mushroom in milk, causing it to ferment, and thus obtain a drink which makes nearly all of them live to be a hundred. A small piece, eaten at the right moment, will save you from death. Moreover, its magic power can provide you with all you wish for. Now, depart in peace.' And he placed his hands on their foreheads.

Antranik and Simitrol thanked the magician and boarded the ship, whose name, *Ararat*, sparkled in the sunshine. What a lucky omen! The crossing was made without incident, and one week later the boat drew into the barbarian shore. The horses were waiting patiently for them on the beach, their noses deep in a sack of fine oats. The two men greeted their mounts with pats and friendly slaps. They found a little cove between high rocks where they could hide the boat after taking from it all they needed for their journey.

Back on the beach they thought out their next step and decided that the best plan was to keep to the coast for as long as they could. So, leaping into

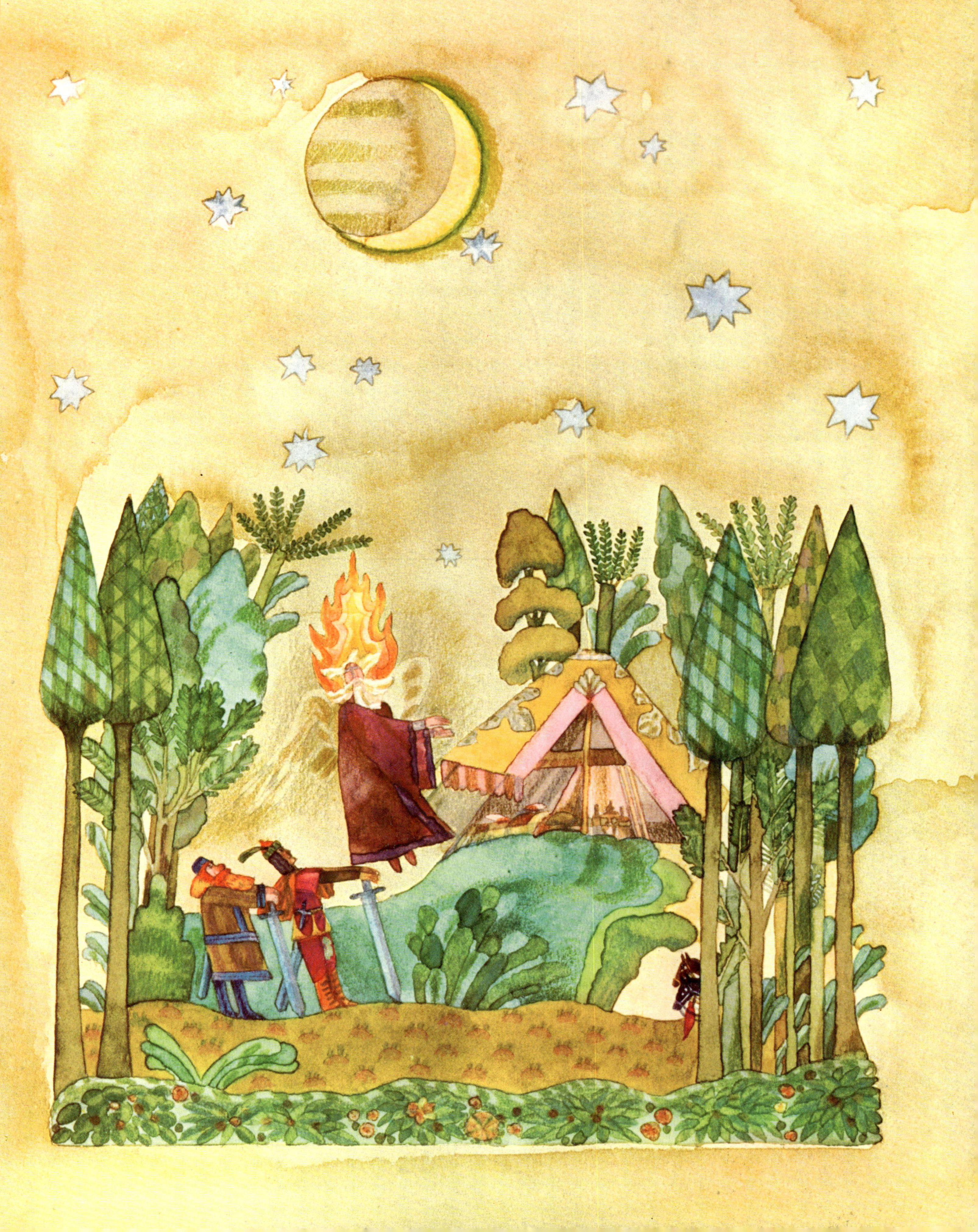

the saddle, they rode on. It was the end of April, and springtime was radiant. The track ran along by the Black Sea – whose waters were the most innocent blue. Our two friends rode through the wildest country, while thousands of birds kept them company with their singing. There was not a house to be seen. The land seemed to be uncultivated. Only after a long week of riding did they catch sight of a poor cottage hidden in a grove of oak trees. Riding up they knocked at the door. After a few minutes a very old woman with a black kerchief tied under her chin opened the door a little way.

'Who are you? Where do you come from?' she asked mistrustfully.

'We are simple travellers from the other side of the sea, and we would like water for ourselves and our horses,' replied Antranik.

'I can see you are not from these parts . . . Sit down, I will fetch you some fresh water.'

While they were drinking, the old woman told them the following story:

'This region is dangerous, you must understand. Very often bandits come and attack us poor people who are trying to raise our cattle. They steal our goats and sheep, kill the shepherds and make off with the women. Further on live barbarians who strike terror through the land. My husband and I are Armenians, so we are Christians. We used to live at Dikranaguerd with our two sons and their families. We were obliged to flee, for these barbarians threatened to force our sons to join their cruel army of mercenaries. We brought away our herds and all the food we could, camping at night in tents. But misfortune followed us. Two of our grandchildren died, of dysentery. Then one night those vile brigands stole away our two daughters-in-law. We still had our sons but they immediately set off to recover their wives. We have never seen them again. My husband and I reached this hut but a week ago and he died of exhaustion and despair at once. Now I am alone, and have lost all those who were dear to me.'

'I feel for you in your sorrow, sincerely,' cried Antranik. He chewed a little piece of the famous mushroom and made appear before the old woman a table loaded with meats, fruits and drinks, while for the horses there were two buckets of oats which they fell upon eagerly. Then, while they all refreshed themselves, the young Prince told his story.

The next day their hostess said to them, 'You have accomplished half your journey but your troubles are not yet over. You must do everything possible to avoid the soldiers of these parts, for there are none more cruel in all the world. Continue to follow the coast to beyond Trebizond. Now go, and may God protect you.' Then she made the sign of the cross on their foreheads.

The travellers gave a last wave of their hands in farewell and set out again on their journey. They walked for a long time and one morning came in sight of a town, doubtless the Samsun of today. Simitrol immediately dismounted, but Antranik, more cautious, held him back. They only just had time to take cover in a thicket of cork trees when they saw a troop of helmeted horsemen come galloping out of Samsun in their direction. The horsemen passed very close, brandishing scimitars and yelling in some strange language. To the girths of the last horses were tied poor wretches whose broken bodies bounced on the rocks in the road. Presently their cries ceased. Only the shouts of the barbarians could be heard, and Antranik realized that their unhappy victims must be dead.

Pursuing their journey, a few miles further on they found a blue river barring their way, too deep to cross on horseback. This was the River Halys. So Antranik ate a little piece of the mushroom and a single wish transported himself and his squire and the two animals to the far bank of the Halys.

In spite of the advice of the old woman, Antranik preferred to avoid the too famous city of Trebizond, and followed the course of a little river, the

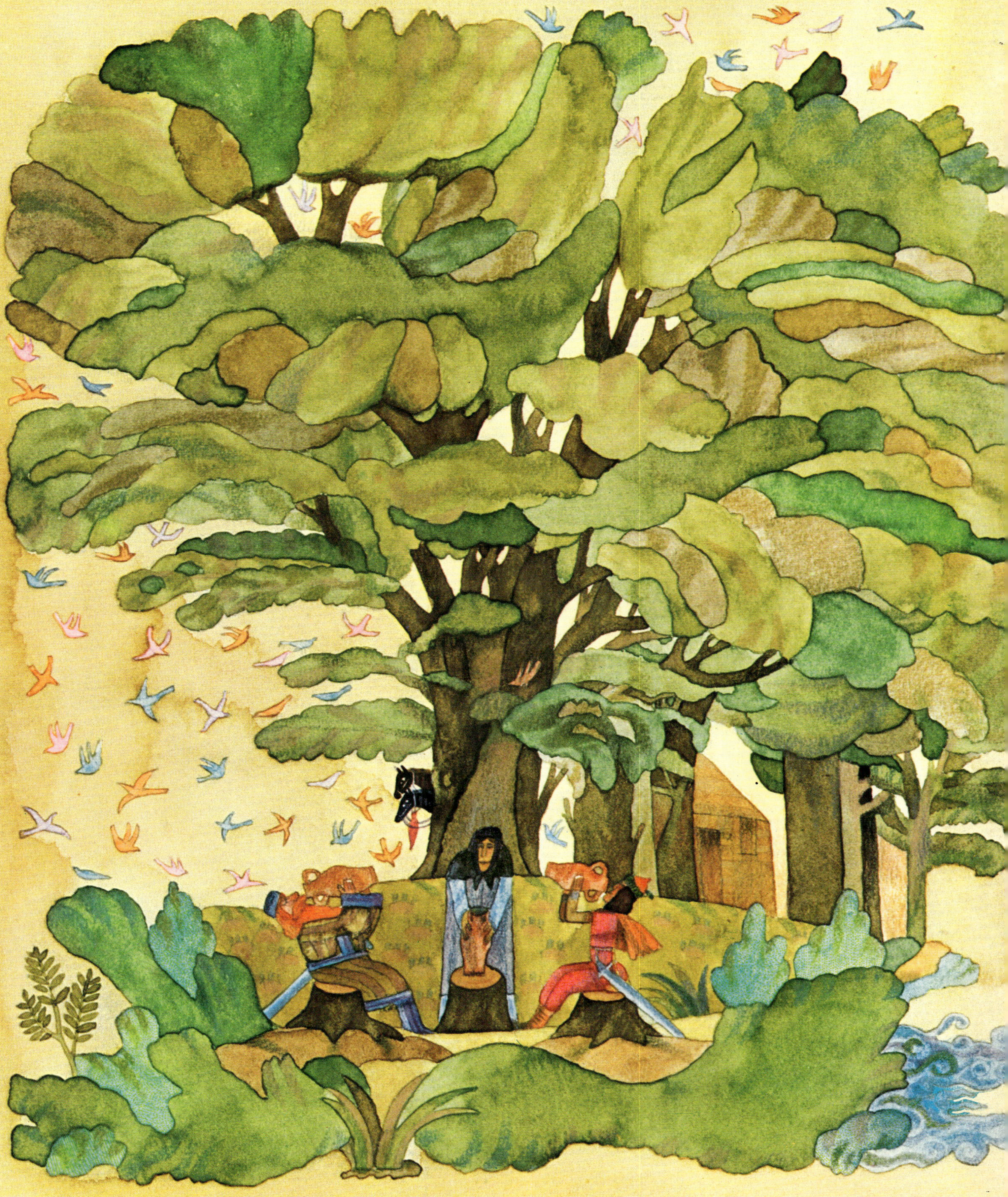

Coruh, by which they were hoping to make their way deep into this mountainous country. And true enough, the stony path which ran beside the stream soon rose very steeply and the horses began to show signs of fatigue. By the evening the little caravan had reached a plateau thick with trees and there they made camp for the night.

The next day was passed in much the same way as they continued their tiring, monotonous climb. Not a single person did they see. Simitrol grew more and more silent and sad, so his master urged him to hum some of the songs from their country. A little reluctantly Simitrol sang some of the quick, lively tunes from the kingdom of Aldebrank, and managed to cheer the party. They went on thus for several days. The track would climb to one ridge and from there would go on to scale yet another height. At last, the travellers found themselves on the banks of another river which the old geographer had named the Euphrates and which, at this point, was not at all like the wide river that flows into the Persian Gulf. It was more like a mountain torrent for they were near the source. After walking on a while longer, Antranik found a place that was narrower with low banks where they could cross the river. Once across the Euphrates the caravan continued its slow progress. The air was quite cold at this altitude and the landscape had changed. The mountain slopes were covered with dry vegetation and in the distance wild goats could be seen leaping from rock to rock.

Three more days of their tiring march and our friends stood gazing at the domes of Erzerum. The belfries of the Armenian churches sparkled in the sun. But the ramparts of the town, built of dried mud, had a distinctly hostile look. The two men slept for a few hours before continuing towards the walls of Erzerum. Entering the town through a broken gate, they saw that the main street was lined with the workshops of coppersmiths who were making a deafening noise with their hammers. By asking a question at the top of his voice Antranik learned that a pedlar at the far end of Erzerum might be able to procure him two mules.

He found the pedlar and told him his whole story. The pedlar scratched his head, embarrassed, and at last declared: 'You are lucky because I'm Armenian. For us the Mystic Mountain of Ararat is a holy mountain. So, although my mules are necessary for my work, I'll gladly give them to you.'

The Prince thanked him and put into his hand a purse full of gold pieces. Then he proposed that they should leave the two horses with the pedlar during the rest of their journey. When they came back they would return the mules and pick up the horses. Simitrol therefore took Chernego and the bay horse to the pedlar's house, who gave him the mules, a pair of fine, black-coated animals.

Antranik declared himself enchanted, and the two men set off happily on their journey. The mules did not travel fast but walked steadily, never slipping on the pebbles. And the Lord knows there were enough pebbles, for the tracks consisted of nothing else in those parts. Simitrol had brought along goat's cheese, some *erchig*, a spiced ham with garlic, and *lavache* bread, as flat as a piece of paper. They stopped only once or twice a day to eat and drink. And day followed day and mile followed mile, marked by the rhythm of the mules' paces.

One morning, when the two men woke they could hardly believe their eyes: a heavy layer of snow lay upon the slopes they had to climb. But, as Antranik said to his squire, they were ten thousand feet up, so snow was normal there, even in the month of June. They went on their way, climbing up and up, higher and higher. It took them several days to get used to the altitude. The air was of a rare purity, and the snow sparkled in the sunlight.

At last one evening, after feeding and watering the mules, the two men were preparing to slip into their sleeping-bags when Simitrol suddenly cried, 'Look, Master – over there, a star, on the ground!'

And indeed there was a light glowing on the ground which, when Antranik went up close, seemed to him to be a luminous circle, as if fifty candles had been lit – yet there was no candle! Antranik stuck a branch in the ground beside it to mark the spot and said, 'We shall see tomorrow.'

He woke before dawn, and ran to where he had stuck the branch in the ground the night before. It was still there, but the light had disappeared. In its place he saw a huge circle cut into the snow. He fell to his knees and began reciting the Christian prayers he had learnt in his father's kingdom. Antranik called his squire and they prayed together. Then they began to clear away the snow from the circle and dig. After a few hours the Prince felt something hard which turned out to be a rectangular block of wood. With the greatest care he lifted out the precious object. He had just time to discern a shape in the ground like a primitive boat when the snow rushed back into the hole and covered everything up again. A voice that seemed to come from the mountain spoke these words: 'Man, you have reached the

goal you set yourself. Go back to your own country and live according to God's laws.' Antranik and Simitrol bowed their heads in awe and gratitude and remained uttering prayers of thanks until the sun was high. Then they made their preparations for departure, the mules were given a triple ration of oats and they started home.

Antranik tore up one of his beautiful Chinese silk shirts, so as to wrap the precious relic of the ark in it, and carried it slung across his chest. He felt magically protected. The mules travelled fast – so much so indeed that scarcely three days later they reached Erzerum. The Prince dashed straight to the house of the man who had lent him the mules, but found nothing there but a pile of charred stones.

'Are you looking for the Armenian?' inquired a neighbour. 'The military wanted to take his three sons away, and he tried to stop them, with the result that the barbarians set fire to his house, killed him and rode off with the horses they heard whinnying in the stables.'

'Heavens! My Chernego!' cried the Prince, horrified.

But after a few moments' thought, he decided that the best plan was to get down to the sea as quickly as he could. So the next day at dawn Antranik and his faithful squire mounted their mules and left Erzerum – though Antranik's heart was heavy at leaving behind in this wild country the horses that had served them so well.

Now the long trek through the mountains began again, from one valley to the next, but this time the route descended all the way, which was much less tiring than the outward journey had been.

One evening they stopped for the night in the shelter of a wood. Suddenly they heard shouts. Simitrol slipped noiselessly through the trees. He was soon back, very excited. 'M-m-master! I've just seen Chernego . . . and my horse, too! There are people there, fighting . . .'

The Prince followed him and in a clearing not far away saw four men quarrelling. Two of them seemed peaceable enough but the other two were shouting at them until, without warning, they threw themselves upon the first two, waving their scimitars in the air. At once the Prince and Simitrol brandished their swords and rushed to the defence of the men who were being attacked. At the first sword-blow they disarmed the attackers. The two others then told their story. They had gone in search of their wives who had been carried off by the barbarians and they had ended by being caught themselves by the soldiers who had been robbing and pillaging throughout the whole region of Erzerum.

'Those are our horses,' said Antranik, 'but from what you say you must surely be the Armenians whose mother was kind to us. Your father is dead, alas, but your mother will be overjoyed to see you again.' The young men wept on hearing this sad news.

The Prince said to them, 'We'll send these scoundrels packing. They shall go on foot, and you can take our mules so as to get back quickly to your mother.'

The soldiers shouted and complained more loudly than ever, but in vain. After the most friendly goodbyes, Antranik and his squire saw the young Armenians on their way before resuming their own journey. The horses had grown thinner but they were glad to see their beloved masters. A week later, after following the green valley of the River Kelkit, they came to Amassia where for a few pieces of silver an old man took them across the ford. Trusting his experience now, Antranik avoided the townships and the camps of the nomads. They marched thus as far as the River Kisilirmak where the Prince decided to rest for a few hours. They bathed, supped, then slept the whole night through. In the morning they felt stronger and went on in good heart.

In the distance they saw Karabuk, then Bolu. At last they found themselves in the valley of the Sakarya, a rich valley, full of the most beautiful trees. Then, following the river they came again to the Black Sea which they had left so many days before. It was still as blue as ever. Now they had to find their boat. Antranik gave each of the horses a tiny bit of mushroom and said, 'Eat that and wait for us on the other side of the water.' Instantly the horses disappeared.

Simitrol and the Prince now went in search of their boat and they soon found the sheltered cove where it lay. They were just climbing aboard when they heard wild cries. Above them, high up on the bank, were about fifty men on horseback, wearing helmets and armed with scimitars. They shouted at them, threatening and cursing. 'Those are the ones . . . they stole our horses . . . We'll kill them!' they yelled, dashing down to the water's edge.

Meanwhile Antranik and his squire, installed in their boat, *Ararat*, rowed as fast as they could. They had already gone some distance from the bank when the leader of the band yelled, 'I want them alive! Everybody into the water!'

The horses plunged in and started to swim in pursuit of the boat, urged on fiercely by their riders. Antranik watched them anxiously as they came gradually closer and closer. What could he do? Desperately he wondered how he could rid himself of his pursuers. Then suddenly an idea came to him, a mad idea, of getting rid of all of them at once. 'This Armenian mushroom . . . it curdles milk! I could try that!'

Taking the mushroom in his hand, he gave a mighty throw and hurled it into the sea in front of his pursuers, shouting, 'Alexiano-Vocheyin! Come to my aid!'

Instantly between the *Ararat* and the barbarian bank the sea became solid, the horses and their riders caught in the mass of solid water, unable to move head or foot, the men shouting, the horses whinnying wildly. Antranik and Simitrol at last reached the Bielogastan shore where the magician himself was waiting for them, beside the horses. The two men thanked him with all their hearts for his miraculous aid.

'You owe me nothing, it was you who saved me. I want to help you once more. There is trouble here in Bielogastan at this moment. So you must sleep one more night in the forest and tomorrow when you wake you will be home in your own country.'

The two companions went to sleep. At dawn they woke and found themselves in front of the palace of Ispalanograd, their home. The servants, seeing two such hairy and travel-stained men, would not allow them into the palace. They fetched Balthegor who, recovering quickly from his first surprise, recognized his brother by his voice. He took him into the King's room where Aldebrank, pale and weak, lay in his canopied bed.

Antranik went down on his knees, untied the relic and placed his father's hand upon it. Instantly, Aldebrank opened his eyes and the colour returned to his cheeks.

'A miracle!' he cried. 'I feel strong and well – and so hungry, I am literally dying of starvation!'

Then, seeing Antranik at the foot of his bed, he burst out laughing. 'Who is this hairy fellow? Can it be my younger son?'

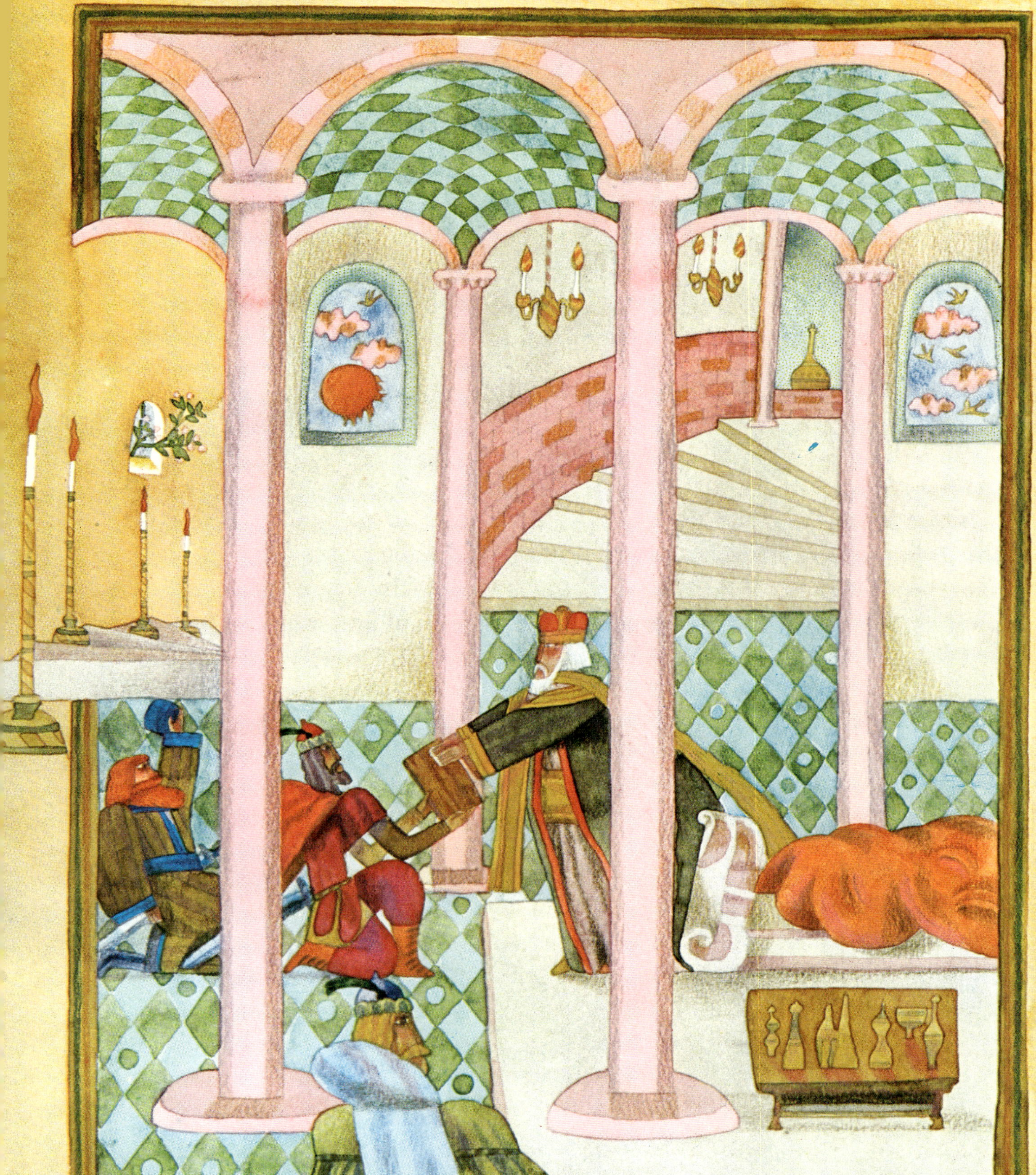

Everybody wept for joy and they all kissed each other. For a whole month there were rejoicings, balls and feasts, feasts, balls and rejoicings, one after the other, without end. The relic from the ark was placed in a special niche in the King's room, with golden lamps beside it that burned day and night. The King lived for many more years to enjoy the companionship of his loving sons! During the long winter evenings, when people were a little bored in the palace, there was always some lively member of the company who would ask: 'Antranik, tell us about your journey to the Mystic Mountain.'

And Antranik never waited to be asked twice. He was happy to tell over and over again the story of his search for Ararat and of all the adventures he had shared with his faithful squire, Simitrol.